"I'd like to see the Head Scientist, please," Eddy said politely.

"You . . . what? The Head Scientist?" the woman said, staring at the Green Grood nervously. "He's gone . . . that is . . . is there something I can do to . . . help you?"

The Grood was reaching for the receptionist's typewriter.

"No, I don't think so, Ma'am," Eddy said, grabbing the Grood's arms. "I need somebody who understands how to fix space machines. See, my Uncle Sedrick got sent into outer space, and if I can't get him back by tomorrow at three o'clock, he'll disappear forever."

CHRISTIAN ADVENTURE SERIES

EDDY
and His Amazing Pet

Michael P. Waite

Chariot Books
David C. Cook Publishing Co.

For Kelly Ann Hinds
who had the frightful misfortune
of growing up with a
Domestic Green Grood
for a brother

Chariot Books is an imprint of David C. Cook Publishing Co.
David C. Cook Publishing Co., Elgin, Illinois 60120
David C. Cook Publishing Co., Weston, Ontario

Cover illustration by Jill Colbert Trousdale

First Printing, 1988
Printed in the United States of America
93 92 91 5 4 3 2

Library of Congress Cataloging-in-Publication Data
Waite, Michael P., 1960—
Eddy and his amazing pet / Michael P. Waite.
p. cm.
Summary: A rude boy who regards neither rules nor the feelings of others changes his ways after he takes care of a pet from outer space who ignores all of his instructions.
[1. Conduct of life—Fiction. 2. Science fiction.] I. Title.
PZ7.W1333Ed 1988 [Fic]—dc19 88-16961
ISBN 1-55513-641-9

Contents

CAMP
TOMAHAWK
OFFICE

1
Good Riddance!

Eddy Hooper sat underneath the big Camp Tomahawk sign flicking pebbles into the woods. He sprawled out on top of his duffel bag and tried to think up excuses to give his parents. Lately, though, they had seemed pretty sick of his excuses. And this time it was almost a lost cause. Mr. Burke, the camp director, had already phoned his parents and told them everything.

Camp Tomahawk was supposed to last all summer long, but Eddy was being sent home after only five days. Not that he cared. The place seemed more like a prison to him. Every time you turned around, they smacked you with another rule. No goofing around. No spitting. No practical jokes.

What a bore!

Looking back, Eddy still couldn't see what was so awful about what he'd done. He had gone to camp to have fun, but every time he tried, it just got him deeper into trouble.

Right off, on the first day of camp, he'd been kicked off the waterfront for practicing his "long distance diving." It seemed like a pretty outrageous penalty for such a minor offense. All he had done was jump from the shower house roof over three canoes into the swimming area. But that was all it took. There were no warnings or anything; the lifeguard just pointed toward the shores and shouted, "GO!"

Then, two days later, the same thing happened at the archery range. Eddy got booted out just for breaking one silly little nitpicky rule: Campers Will Shoot Only One Arrow at a Time. But who takes rules like *that* seriously? Besides, he was just joking around, trying to have a little fun. He wanted to see what would happen if he fired six arrows at once, and *TWANG*!—off they went, swerving through the air like a flock of runaway missiles. One landed in the tennis courts, two disappeared into the woods, one hit a target (over in the rifle range), and one went through the roof of Mr. Burke's private golf cart. The archery instructor suspended Eddy for the rest of the week because of "unsafe conduct" and "for being an all-around smarty-pants." Can you imagine that? They actually had a rule against being a "smarty-pants"!

After lots of lectures, warnings, punishments, and so on, Eddy had decided to watch his step for a while. And he was doing fairly well until one day in nature class.

Right from the beginning, he had despised nature class—mostly because it was taught by Mrs. Pottswell, who had also been his science teacher last year in school. She had made Eddy's whole year a dreadful nightmare, and just to top it off, she had given him a D minus on his report card. So you can imagine, he wasn't too happy when she showed up at Camp Tomahawk as the nature counselor—it was as though she was following him around just to make his life miserable. But now, in summer vacation, Eddy was not much in the mood to be bossed around by some old schoolteacher with a bunch of fuddy-duddy rules. So he made up his mind to simply ignore her—that is, until The Big Disaster happened.

It had been Eddy's turn to clean the fish tanks, and Mrs. Pottswell had given him specific orders *not* to touch Rex, the snapping turtle. But Eddy just couldn't help himself. After all, how often do you get to play with a snapping turtle? Almost never! Eddy just wanted to tease Rex a little bit by holding him over the trout tank, that's all. Unfortunately, the second that Rex got one sniff of those tasty little fish, he went absolutely *nutso*, and there was nothing Eddy could do to stop him. (Would you want to stick your fingers into a fish tank with a freaked-out snapping turtle?)

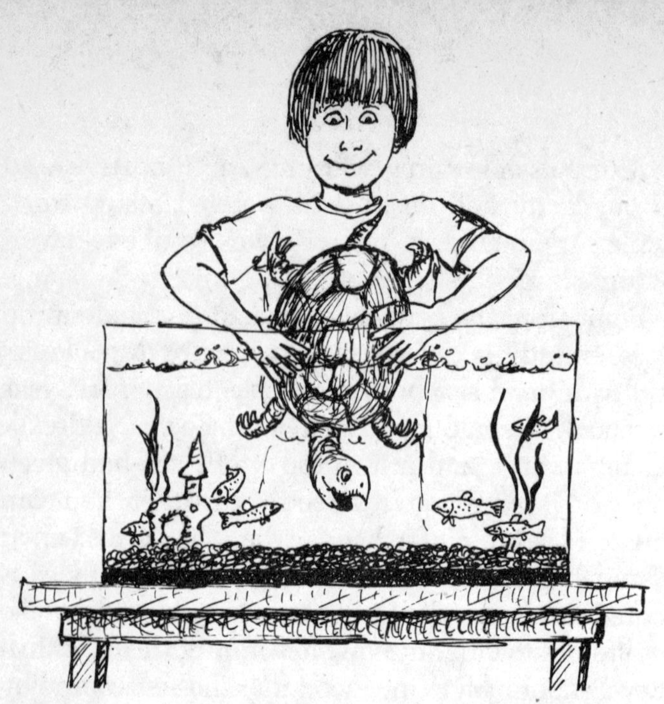

When it was all over, the aquarium was scattered across the nature room floor in a thousand tiny pieces. The carpet was a sopping bog of mud and algae. And Rex had polished off seven baby brook trout.

Mrs. Pottswell showed up just as Eddy was trapping Rex in a garbage can. She dragged him straight to Mr. Burke's office, and a few minutes later they had Eddy's parents on the telephone. With all parties agreeing it would be the best thing for Camp Tomahawk, Eddy Hooper was being sent home first thing in the morning.

So now, an hour after leaving camp, Eddy was still sitting beneath the Camp Tomahawk sign, and his parents were nowhere to be seen. He had run out of things to do to distract himself—catching bugs, weaving potholders out of grass, building twig villages—and now he found himself worrying. Perhaps his parents had gotten into an accident. Or maybe they had completely forgotten to come get him. Or maybe they had just decided to leave him out in the woods to fend for himself (they *did* seem to be rather sick of him lately). But fortunately, none of these answers was true. Just then he heard the loud whir of a motor coming toward him. It sounded too loud to be his parents' car, but Eddy stared down the road anyway.

Around the corner came an old motorcycle with a sidecar. A heavyset man in an orange raincoat was driving, and he rumbled right up in front of Eddy, then stopped. A big mop of silver hair popped out of the helmet, joined by a round, jolly face wearing purple sunglasses. Eddy jumped to his feet in surprise.

"Uncle Sedrick!" he shouted. "What are *you* doing here?"

"Ah! Hello!" Uncle Sedrick smiled. "Been waiting long?"

"Yeah, practically forever," Eddy said, staring curiously at the motorcycle. "Where's Mom and Dad?"

"Europe," Uncle Sedrick said. "Your grandma took ill, I'm afraid, and your parents decided to leave for England right away. They asked me to come fetch you and keep you at my house for a week or two. I hope you don't mind. So, anyway, here I am. I hear you've got yourself kicked out of camp, eh?"

"Some camp!" Eddy sneered. "It's more like a jailhouse. Every time you try to have some fun, they tell you it's against the rules. You wouldn't believe it, Uncle Sedrick—it's worse than school!"

Eddy liked his Uncle Sedrick a great deal—Sedrick wasn't bossy like most adults. In fact, he even used to let Eddy play with one of his best telescopes (that is, until Eddy dropped it off the roof by mistake). Eddy's dad always called Uncle Sedrick "that crazy old astronomer," because his house was so full of gadgets . . . and because Uncle Sedrick *was* just a little *different*. But to Eddy, the idea of staying at Uncle Sedrick's house for a couple of weeks was a welcome rescue. By the time Mom and Dad got back from Europe, the whole thing with Camp Tomahawk would be ancient history and he would probably escape punishment altogether.

"That's my nephew," Uncle Sedrick said with a sigh. "You haven't changed a bit. Ever since you were the size of a toadstool, you've always hated rules."

"That's 'cause they're stupid," Eddy said, throwing his duffel bag into the sidecar.

"Well, I don't mean to be contrary," Uncle Sedrick said. "But you must remember, it was God who came up with the idea of rules in the first place.

I don't think He was trying to ruin our fun, though . . . just trying to protect us from hurting each other, if you see what I mean. And from hurting *ourselves* for that matter."

"Gimme a break, Uncle Sedrick," Eddy groaned. "I'm really sick of all this rule stuff. Besides, it's not God's fault that people make up dumb rules. It's people like Mrs. Pottswell who go around tryin' to ruin everybody's life."

"Well, you know, . . ." Uncle Sedrick started to say, but Eddy gave him a disgusted glance, which obviously meant "End of Discussion." Uncle Sedrick breathed a sigh of defeat and climbed back onto the motorcycle.

Eddy got into the sidecar and fixed his gaze down the empty road. He was angry and frustrated with Camp Tomahawk, and talking about it just made things worse. It seemed as if the whole world was trying to order him around and make his life as boring as possible. And there was no point in arguing. No one ever understood. He just wanted to get away from everyone from Mrs. Pottswell and Mr. Burke and all their confining rules—and go someplace where no one would bother him. *There's got to be someplace like that*, Eddy thought. *Maybe on another planet or something.*

Uncle Sedrick started up the motorcycle and spun it around in the middle of the road. The Camp Tomahawk sign disappeared in a cloud of dust and gravel. And soon the campgrounds were far behind.

Eddy sat back in the sidecar and let the wind flutter against his face. Dark evergreens flickered past on both sides of the road like pictures in a movie. He was safe now. His troubles were over.

"So long, Camp Tomahawk," Eddy whispered to himself. "And good riddance!"

2
The Toy from Planet Zerb

Uncle Sedrick's house was at the very top of Bald Rock Hill overlooking the town of Puttford. It was one of those spooky old houses with lots of gables and towers. But Uncle Sedrick had cut away part of the roof to make room for his gigantic telescope. And scattered across the rooftop were various satellite dishes, antennae, and all sorts of radar equipment. So now it looked like a haunted house that had been taken over by Martians.

Eddy came to visit Uncle Sedrick for a couple weeks every summer, and one of his favorite pastimes was exploring the house. It was a huge maze full of hiding spots, secret rooms, and winding staircases. He could explore for days and never grow bored. And that's exactly what he was thinking

about as he hurried up the walkway to the front door.

"Slow down a minute!" Uncle Sedrick called, blocking Eddy's path with a raincoat sleeve. "Now, Eddy," he said. "You know that I don't usually have lots of rules in my house. . . ."

"Yeah, that's what I like about this place," said Eddy glancing through the door anxiously.

"Well, I'm glad you like it here," Uncle Sedrick went on, though Eddy wasn't paying attention. "But things are a little different this time. You see, I'm working on a special project—an extremely *dangerous* one—and it's very important that you don't go playing around with it . . . or something awful could happen! But that's the only big rule I have. So, do you think you could go along with it?"

"Sure," Eddy said. "One rule's no big deal. It's just that places like Camp Tomahawk have rules for everything. Stupid ones, too."

"Oh, my goodness!" Uncle Sedrick started, looking down at his watch. "It's almost three o'clock! Follow me, Eddy. . . . I'll show you this project I was talking about. But remember what I said—very, *very* dangerous! Please, Eddy, I couldn't be more serious."

Uncle Sedrick hurried inside, tearing off his raincoat anxiously. He charged through the hallway and turned immediately up a staircase that was so narrow he barely fit. Eddy followed him, taking three steps at a time. He expected that this project must be pretty spectacular, and he was already wondering how he could help out. Three flights up, the stairway ended in Uncle Sedrick's research room—a long, open space which, at one time, had been an attic. It was crammed full of electronic equipment, telescopes, radios, charts, file cabinets, and other sorts of scientific clutter. Eddy followed his uncle to the far end of the room where a strange machine stood on the floor. This machine was made up of a tall glass case surrounded by computer parts and a tangle of wires. The case was almost as big as a closet, so, of course, Eddy's first impulse was to open the glass door and step inside.

"Ho there!" cried Uncle Sedrick, grabbing Eddy by the shoulder. "Now this is what I was telling you! You've got to be careful here—this is a very dangerous machine."

"It looks like a big electric fish tank to me," Eddy said smugly.

"Hmm," said Uncle Sedrick, stepping back from his contraption. "So it does! But, no matter—that's not what it is. It's an Interplanetary Object Exchange Machine. I use it to send things from earth up to a planet called Zerboglatus Five—that's *Planet Zerb* for short. And they send things from their planet down to me. Fascinating, eh?"

"Yeah, right!" Eddy said doubtfully. "There's no such thing as a planet called Zergobottomus."

"Planet Zerb," Uncle Sedrick corrected him. "And in precisely seven minutes you shall see that there is indeed a Planet Zerb!"

"How?" said Eddy.

"Because I'm going to exchange an earth-object for a Zerb-object," Uncle Sedrick explained. "And today the object is a common toy. I'm sending a toy airplane."

"Can I work some of the buttons?" said Eddy, stepping toward the machine again.

"No, I'm afraid not," Uncle Sedrick said, stopping him in midstep. "In fact, it would probably be best if you just sat down and watched."

"Aw, come on, Uncle Sedrick!"

"I really must insist," said Uncle Sedrick. And he cleared off a tabletop for Eddy to sit on.

Eddy plopped onto the table with a loud sigh of disgust and began playing with whatever he could reach. Meanwhile, Uncle Sedrick raced about the room flicking switches, adjusting knobs, and checking gauges, all of which he did at an incredible speed. Finally, he placed a red plastic airplane inside the glass case and shut thc door.

A timer at thc top of thc machine began counting down from sixty seconds. The machine began humming softly and a row of green lights above the doorway began to flash. And just as the timer struck zero, Uncle Sedrick pulled down a lever beside the word *ignition*.

Then he stood back to watch.

"Now, in order for the exchange to work," Uncle Sedrick explained, smiling proudly, "my friend on

Planet Zerb has programmed his machine to operate at the exact same time as mine. If one of our machines isn't functioning, then nothing will happen. Also, each of our Transport Boxes must contain an object that we intend to exchange—that's what the toy airplane is for. Two objects must be exchanged at once, you see, or the machine won't work. Last of all, we pull the ignition levers—which I have already done—and everything's ready to go. The exchange should happen any second now!"

But for a very long time nothing happened. The green lights over the doorway continued flashing as before. The machine whirred and growled and clicked and clattered. But the toy airplane stayed right where it was. Eddy's doubts began to grow and Uncle Sedrick began to look more concerned by the moment.

Then, just as Eddy was thinking about going to get himself a snack, a loud bell went off. The green lights turned to red and began blinking. And in another moment, the toy airplane vanished with a flash. Eddy stared breathlessly at the empty case: one second passed, two, three, four, five, and *ZAP*! —a strange, colorful object appeared right where the toy airplane had been before.

"Wow!" exclaimed Eddy, jumping to his feet.

"Excellent," commented Uncle Sedrick. He opened the glass door and removed the toy.

It was evidently a ball of some sort. It was bright

yellow, round, and covered with spongy little bumps. There was a note attached, which Uncle Sedrick read quickly and stuffed into his shirt pocket. He studied the ball for a moment longer, then gave it a bounce against the floor. As soon as the ball struck the carpet a soft, pleasant tune began to play. The ball continued bouncing to the rhythm of the music with no one having to help it along at all. Each time it bounced into the air at exactly the same height. And, at last, when the song ended, the ball fell softly to the floor and went motionless. Eddy picked up the ball to try it for himself. He gave it a much harder bounce and the ball went all the way to the ceiling. Also, a much faster, louder song came out, and when the song ended, once again, the ball dropped to the floor and became instantly still.

"Absolutely amazing," said Uncle Sedrick, picking up the ball to study it.

"Yeah," gasped Eddy. "That's gotta be the coolest ball anywhere. I wonder what kind of sports they play with it."

Uncle Sedrick took the note out of his pocket for a second reading.

"What's it say?" asked Eddy, peering over his uncle's shoulder.

"It's from my friend, Yibbig," Uncle Sedrick said. "He was the first one I contacted on Planet Zerb—quite by mistake I might add. He had built a similar machine to this one, and we were both testing them

at the same time when—surprise!—we just happened to connect. At any rate, I sent Yibbig an English dictionary and he learned the entire language in less than a week! At the same time, he sent me a Zerboglatian dictionary . . . but I can't make heads or tails of the thing. I'd show it to you, but it disappeared. Things do that, I'm afraid —after about twenty-four hours, things from Planet Zerb simply vanish. Yibbig has the same problem with things from earth. We can't figure out what causes it."

"So, anyway, what's the note say?" Eddy said anxiously.

"Ah, yes," Uncle Sedrick said, opening the note. "Short as usual." And here is what he read:

> *CORRESPONDENCE DATE:* Vargomid 56th, Year of Kernik D#6792
>
> *TO:* Dr. Sedrick F. Heisenburg of Planet Earth
>
> Dear Sedrick,
>
> I hope you enjoy this toy Poinkaverp (I don't know what the English word would be). It bounces and plays music simultaneously—it's quite a fad here on Zerboglatus Five. I look forward to seeing your earth toy as well. It's terribly sad that these things will only last a day or so before

disintegrating—I am still trying to figure out why this happens.

Tomorrow at 3 p.m. we will exchange common house pets as we discussed previously. (I have not decided what to send to you yet—do you already have Pink-Snouted Viggworts on earth?) Then, at 4 p.m. we shall return the pets to each other (as we also discussed) to prevent them from disintegrating. I look forward to this experiment with great anticipation. Until then, oozing heaps of mud on your shoes!

Your friend,

Yibbig of Planet Zerb

"What's that mean—'Mud on your shoes'?" said Eddy.

"Oh, that's just a sort of expression they have on Planet Zerb," Uncle Sedrick explained. "It's like saying 'Have a nice day' or 'Best wishes' . . . that kind of thing."

"Must be a weird planet," Eddy deduced.

Uncle Sedrick studied the Zerboglatian toy for a while, then gave it a gentle bounce. As a soft tune began to play and the ball began moving to the rhythm, Uncle Sedrick suddenly turned to Eddy with a huge smile of delight.

"Tomorrow will be the grandest day yet, Eddy!"

he said. "Tomorrow afternoon at 3 p.m. right here in my own house, a miracle will happen! First, I will place a small kitten inside the Transport Box of my Exchange Machine. Then I will set the controls into operation, and presto!—the kitten will be gone. But a moment later, Eddy—this is the best part—just a moment later, a small animal from Planet Zerb will appear in the kitten's place! And that animal will become the first creature from outer space to ever enter the earth's atmosphere. As far as we know, that is."

Eddy let out a sharp whistle. "Gosh, Uncle Sedrick," he gasped. "What do you think it'll be? What if it's a space monster . . . like a dragon that shoots lasers or somethin'?"

Uncle Sedrick laughed. "I don't think so, Eddy," he said. "Yibbig is a brilliant scientist. I don't think he'd play such an awful trick. I imagine he'll send something cute and fluffy . . . perhaps they have different types of kittens and puppies on Planet Zerb. Who knows?"

"Well, maybe," Eddy said. "But I've heard about lots of space creatures and none of 'em were ever cute and fluffy."

"Just think of it, Eddy," Uncle Sedrick continued, ignoring his nephew's dark visions. "Tomorrow at this time, we'll be in the presence of an animal from another galaxy. Won't it be marvelous? Today, a toy from Planet Zerb . . . and tomorrow, a living creature!"

3
Eddy Helps Out

Eddy was so excited about seeing what sort of pet would come from Planet Zerb that he could think of nothing else all day long. The morning seemed to drag on for eternity. Uncle Sedrick wouldn't even let him into the research room until everything was ready—which looked like it was going to be never. So Eddy had nothing to do but watch television and snack on junk food. And that's how he spent most of the day. Finally, at quarter to three, Uncle Sedrick came into the room with a big smile of excitement spread across his face.

"Now, remember," Uncle Sedrick said as they climbed the stairway, "same thing as yesterday. This is a very dangerous process, so I don't want you to touch anything. All right?"

"Sure, sure," Eddy agreed, somewhat annoyed.

"It would probably be best if you just sat on the table again until the whole thing is over," Uncle Sedrick added.

"Man," Eddy complained, "this place is gettin' as bad as Camp Tomahawk!"

This rule about sitting on the table was really starting to get on Eddy's nerves. He had been waiting for this big moment since yesterday, and he had hoped that Uncle Sedrick might let him have a small part in the actual exchange process. He wasn't asking for much, just a chance to pull a couple levers or something. But, no. Instead, he had to sit on a dumb old table and watch while Uncle Sedrick had all the fun. It was really quite unfair, Eddy thought. Why should he be treated like a two-year-old? But there was obviously no point in arguing. The best thing to do, he figured would be to play it cool and hope that Uncle Sedrick would change his mind.

In order to prove that he was actually a serious, self-controlled type of kid, Eddy went directly to the table and sat down. He watched quietly while his uncle made the usual adjustments on the Exchange Machine.

"There," said Uncle Sedrick, with a clap of his hands. "Everything is set to go. Now, in exactly forty-five seconds, all I have to do is pull this ignition switch, and the exchange process will begin. Absolutely exhilarating, isn't it?"

Uncle Sedrick was glowing with delight. The

machine buzzed and crackled. The green lights cast an eerie glimmer throughout the room.

"Thirty seconds and counting!" cheered Uncle Sedrick.

"What about the kitten?" said Eddy. "Aren't you supposed to put the kitten in that big glass box?"

Uncle Sedrick's face turned white as a snowball.

"Oh, my goodness! I've forgotten the kitten!" he cried. And he charged down the stairs at breakneck speed.

Eddy watched the timer counting down the seconds: twenty-six, twenty-five, twenty-four. . . . He wondered if he shouldn't do something. But the only button he knew about was the ignition switch, and that wouldn't help until the kitten was placed inside the glass case.

The timer was down to fourteen when Uncle Sedrick came rumbling back up the stairway. He raced toward the Exchange Machine with the kitten tucked under his arm like a football. He fumbled with the glass door.

Nine, eight, seven . . .

As Uncle Sedrick struggled with the door, the kitten wiggled loose and sprang beneath a computer table. Eddy jumped from the tabletop and watched in horror.

Six, five, four . . .

Uncle Sedrick scooped up the kitten and raced toward the glass Transport Box. The door hung open.

IGNITION
OFF
ON

Three, two . . .

Eddy could no longer contain himself. He jumped toward the Exchange Machine and pulled the ignition switch just as Uncle Sedrick reached the glass door. And at that very moment, his uncle tripped on the toy ball from Planet Zerb and rolled into the Transport Box with a clumsy *THUD*!

One, zero. . . . *FLASH*!

And Uncle Sedrick was gone.

4
The Grood

Eddy stared at the empty Exchange Machine in horror. Quickly, he jerked his hand away from the ignition lever and stumbled backwards. A hot rush of fear swept through his body; his chest tightened with panic. It seemed impossible, unreal. He could not believe what he had just done—Uncle Sedrick was now somewhere in outer space on a planet called Zerboglatus Five.

Then, suddenly, a white flash exploded inside the Exchange Machine compartment . . . and a moment later, a large object appeared.

Eddy ran to open the door, praying that Uncle Sedrick had miraculously returned. But instead, he found a tall, round cage with a very strange animal seated inside. Eddy lifted the cage out of the

Exchange Machine and set it down on the floor.

"OUT!" screamed the creature, jumping to its feet. "GROOD WANT GET OUT!"

Eddy jumped back in surprise. The creature was grasping the bars and glaring at him. It was a strange little animal—comically plump and about the size of a monkey. Its body was covered top to bottom with rough green fur, except for a chimplike face which had big round eyes, a very red nose, and pouty blue lips.

"OUT NOW!" it screamed. And it began jumping up and down inside the cage. Its tantrum grew in force and volume until it seemed as if the creature would hurt itself. Eddy decided he might as well let it out of the cage just to shut it up. His main concern right now was to figure out a way to get Uncle Sedrick back.

As soon as Eddy unlatched the door, the creature leaped out of its cage and plunged headlong through a stack of Uncle Sedrick's paperwork. It bounced off the desktop and landed in a swivel chair. After ten or twelve speeding rotations, it flew out of the chair and ran up to the top of Uncle Sedrick's giant telescope. Finally, it slid down the telescope as if it were a playground slide, rolled over the top of a large computer, and raced down the stairway.

A moment later, Eddy could hear the creature tearing up the downstairs. He considered going down to stop it, but decided to concentrate on getting Uncle Sedrick back instead. Just then, he noticed a note attached to the Zerb creature's cage. He opened it up, and this is what it said:

CORRESPONDENCE DATE: Vargomid 57th, Year of Kernik D#6792

TO: Dr. Sedrick F. Heisenburg, of Planet Earth

Dear Sedrick,

I am sending you a Domestic Green Grood as my example of a common house pet from Zerboglatus Five. I must warn you, the Grood is a very loud, difficult animal, and although it is not dangerous, it should not be let out of its cage under any circumstances (for your own sanity!).

Here on Planet Zerb we use Groods mostly to teach our kids about behavior, responsibility, and so on—unfortunately, you will not have the Grood long enough to employ it for this use.

For your amusement, I have taught the Grood a few sentences of the English language. You see, the Grood is much like the parrots and cockatoos of your planet, and it is able to learn a respectable vocabulary. (It seems to prefer words that describe food and mischief.) I hope the creature doesn't bother you too much. It can be terribly demanding. But no matter, since you will only have to put up with him for one hour.

As we discussed previously, we will set our Exchange Machines to return the pets at precisely 4 p.m. in earth time. I am looking forward to seeing the pet you will send from earth (although my daughter is afraid you will send something like a dragon that shoots laser beams!).

As always, mud on your shoes!

Yibbig of Planet Zerb

As the sounds of destruction grew louder downstairs, Eddy was wishing he had read this note before letting the Grood out of its cage. But a much worse predicament occurred to him just then: If he couldn't figure out how to operate the Exchange Machine by 4 p.m. that afternoon (when the pets were supposed to be returned), Uncle Sedrick could possibly be stuck on Planet Zerb for good. And if Eddy couldn't get the machine to work by this time tomorrow, then Uncle Sedrick would disintegrate!

He stared at the machine blankly. It was so big and complicated—how could he possibly get it to work? And just then the toy ball from Zerb which sat in front of the Exchange Station began to glow. It shimmered a pale white light for several seconds . . . and then, it disappeared. It had disintegrated into thin air.

5
Eddy's Plan

It did not take Eddy very long to realize that the Exchange Machine was much too complex for him to operate. Even though he had found most of Uncle Sedrick's notes and diagrams, there was nothing he could do. They were all written in strange mathematical formulas made up of letters and squiggles.

As far as Eddy could see, there was only one hope left. He had to find another scientist—someone who would be smart enough to understand his uncle's notes and operate the Exchange Machine. Most importantly, Eddy had to find this person *very* soon . . . or else Uncle Sedrick would be no more. He hurried downstairs with an armful of his uncle's notes.

In his panic, he had completely forgotten about the Domestic Green Grood from Planet Zerb. But now, as he started for the kitchen telephone, he was suddenly reminded. The Grood was standing in front of the refrigerator with the door wide open. It had already gathered an enormous pile of food into its arms and was still digging for more.

"Hey, come on!" Eddy shouted. "Get out of there. You've got enough to eat!"

"Grood EAT!" the Grood shouted, and he raced into the living room with his giant load of snacks.

Eddy hurried after him.

"Listen," Eddy said. "You're gonna get sick if you eat all that junk. You'll throw up or something . . . whatever it is that Groods do."

But when he tried to take some of the food away from the Grood, it let out an awful howl and tried to stuff the food under a sofa cushion.

"Go!" it shouted. "Grood EAT!"

Eddy stepped back for fear that the creature would bite him. But instead, it turned its attention to the television remote control. The television popped into activity and the Grood turned the volume all the way up.

"Whoa! That's too loud!" Eddy shouted, amidst the blare of a soda commercial. But when he reached for the TV remote, the Grood squealed louder than ever.

"Go!" it commanded again. "Grood EAT! Grood WATCH! Grood do WHAT GROOD WANT!"

COLA

Eddy threw up his hands and marched out of the room. If the Grood wanted to eat itself to death, then let it! He went to the kitchen and shut the door. The noise from the television rumbled through the walls making the dishes in the cupboard rattle.

He hunted through Uncle Sedrick's kitchen drawers until he found a telephone book. Then he looked up SCIENTISTS in the Yellow Pages, hoping to find someone who would understand his predicament. The only place that sounded worth calling was listed under SCIENTIFIC LABORATORIES. It was a space research center called Baxburg Aeronautics. Eddy went to the phone and dailed.

"Good afternoon, Baxburg Aeronautics," a pleasant-sounding woman greeted him.

"Oh . . . hi," Eddy stammered. "Uh . . . my name's Eddy Hooper and, well, somethin' really weird just happened. See, my Uncle Sedrick built this machine that sends stuff to a planet called Zerboglatus. But, like, he got stuck inside it and I sorta pushed a button and he got sent into outer space. And now I can't get him back, but instead I got this furry green space creature that's called a Grood. I was wonderin' . . . do you have any scientist who could maybe figure out how this machine works and help get my uncle back . . . do you think?"

But when Eddy stopped to wait for her answer, all he got was the buzzing sound of a dead line. The woman had hung up on him. Eddy could see no other route to take, so he dialed again.

"Hello, Baxburg Aeronautics," said the same voice.

"Hi, it's me again," said Eddy. "Please don't hang up . . . 'cause I'm not kiddin', honest. All that stuff I said before really *did* happen. You gotta help me. . . ."

CLICK! went the phone. And then, BZZZZZZZ.

Eddy sat down on the floor to think. He shuffled through the Yellow Pages anxiously, but no new ideas came to him. Baxburg Aeronautics was the only place around that had anything to do with science and outer space. But how could he prove to them that he was telling the truth? They would just think he was making prank calls and hang up again. Unless! Unless he could go there in person and *show* them the Domestic Green Grood from Planet Zerb! Any scientist who took one look at the Grood would instantly know that there was no such creature on earth. Then they would have to believe his story!

The biggest problem now, Eddy realized, would be getting the Grood over to Baxburg Aeronautics. He wasn't sure he could even get the creature back into its cage.

Just then, he noticed that all the noise in the living room had stopped. Evidently, the Grood had shut off the television, and Eddy was afraid to think what the little monster might be doing next. He hurried upstairs to get the cage, praying that the Grood hadn't left the house yet. He could just imagine trying to chase that animal through the forest.

But when he returned to the living room, he found the Grood lying facedown on the carpet. It was groaning and whining and clutching its pudgy little stomach with both hands.

Without warning, Eddy pounced on top of the creature and shoved it into the cage.

"OW," it whimpered. "Grood HURT! Food BAD!"

"Oh, so you ate too much, did you?" Eddy scolded, locking the cage. "I knew you were gonna get sick. But did you listen to me? No, of course not. Maybe you'll pay attention to me next time!"

It occurred to Eddy just then that he was sounding an awful lot like certain adults he knew. So he ended his lecture there and hurried out of the house with the Grood cage. If he was lucky, he could make it to Baxburg Aeronautics before closing time.

6
The Grood Visits Puttford

In the back of Uncle Sedrick's garage, Eddy found an old bicycle. It was a beat-up one-speeder with fat bald tires and a lot of rust. Even so, Eddy knew it would be a great deal better than walking—it was six miles from Uncle Sedrick's house to the town of Puttford, and who could say how much farther it would be to Baxburg Aeronautics?

While the Grood cried and moaned about its sore "tum-tum," Eddy strapped the cage onto the rear fender of the bike. He gathered his uncle's notes together and put them in a rucksack, and soon he was ready to go.

The ride down Bald Rock Hill was a great deal worse than Eddy had imagined. It was a long,

twisting decline with lots of bumps and potholes which made the bicycle shake as if it would fly to pieces at any moment. The Grood didn't help matters much either. It began to screech at an unbearable pitch (one that left Eddy's ears ringing for days), and it bounced from side to side in its cage as if trying to smash its way out.

"You're just making things worse!" Eddy shouted. "If I go off the road, you're gonna get splattered all over the rocks. Can't you see that?"

But, of course, the Grood didn't see. It just shrieked and rampaged all the more, and that's exactly what it planned to do until it could get its own way.

It was quite a sight when Eddy and his furry green passenger came rolling into town on that wobbly old bicycle. Fortunately, the blare and bustle of downtown Puttford was enough to distact the Grood for a while, and it paused from its tantrum in order to stare at the people on the sidewalks. The people stared back with equal interest.

The Grood seemed to be especially entertained by the cars and trucks that were motoring through town. And soon it became impassioned with the idea of climbing into one and going for a ride.

"FAST!" the Grood said, pointing at a station wagon. "Grood want FAST!"

"Sorry," Eddy said. "But I'm going as fast as I can."

"FAST!" the Grood protested, resuming its angry

fits. And it stuck one of its arms through the bars of the cage hoping to find a "FAST" to grab onto.

At just that moment a pickup truck pulled out of a parking space and came alongside Eddy's bike. The Grood's anxious fingers reached out and caught hold of a post on the pickup's tailgate. And suddenly, Eddy felt the bicycle jerk to one side. In an instant, the handlebars twisted sideways and the bike went plunging into a forward somersault. The truck swerved out of the way, and the downtown traffic came to a honking, squealing, skidding halt. Eddy went tumbling onto the pavement and rolled against the curb with a painful SMACK! At the same time, the Grood's cage flew from the back of the bicycle and cracked open against the blacktop. The Grood let out a frightened shriek as it rolled free from the wreckage. It sat in the road bawling for a moment, till suddenly, it realized it was free. Then, with tremendous glee, it jumped to its feet and raced off down the street.

Eddy's head was still spinning when he saw the Grood charging off into the downtown traffic. This time, a number of cars smacked into one another, and several people went off the road just at the sight of the strange green animal. Bruised and dizzy, Eddy got to his feet and hurried after it. There was a jumble of beeping cars for three blocks in every direction.

When Eddy finally caught up with the Grood, it

had climbed to the top of the cereal aisle in Horton's Grocery Market. A crowd of people were gathered below, staring up in wonder as the creature chomped its way through several boxes of Sugar-Coated Fruit Flakes.

"Come down from there!" Eddy commanded. "You're gonna get us both in trouble!"

"NO!" squawked the Grood. "Grood EAT! Do what Grood WANT!"

"You can't do that!" Eddy shouted, quite helplessly. "You aren't allowed to climb on the shelves in stores! And you're especially not supposed to eat stuff you haven't paid for. So get down, right *now*!"

"NO!" the Grood bellowed. "Go 'way! Grood do what Grood WANT!"

Just then Mr. Horton, the store owner, stepped up to Eddy, and he did not look pleased.

"That little green monkey up there . . . or whatever it is," Mr. Horton said, pointing to the Grood. "Is that your pet?"

"Well, sort of," Eddy admitted.

The Grood tore open a box of Chocolate Marshmallow Corn Puffs and began pouring them into its mouth.

"Then please get it down from there immediately, or I shall have to call the police!" Mr. Horton was getting angry.

"Yes, sir," Eddy said. "I'm real sorry about this. . . ."

"Please, son," the grocer said, impatiently. "Just

catch the beast before it destroys my whole store!"

"Yes, sir," Eddy promised and ran around to the backside of the aisle. There in the pet food section, Eddy found a collar and leash designed for small dogs. He thought these items might work for Groods as well, so he tucked them into his pocket for the moment. Then he took a sweatshirt out of his rucksack and climbed up the shelves quietly.

As he peeked over the top shelf, he could see the Grood burying its face inside a cereal box just a few feet away. The creature didn't suspect a thing. Suddenly, Eddy sprang onto the top shelf and threw his sweatshirt over the Grood's head. Then, pinning the little monster to the shelf, he strapped the collar around its neck and attached the leash to the collar. The Grood made a horrible racket, howling and spitting and kicking cereal boxes in every direction. But after a while, it realized it could not escape and stopped fighting in order to whimper and howl.

Eddy climbed down from the shelf, dragging the Grood behind him on the new leash. Together they pushed their way through the crowd, which had grown considerably in both size and bewilderment. Eddy paid Mr. Horton for the collar and leash and promised to come back later to pay for all of the cereal the Grood had destroyed. But Mr. Horton was just glad to get rid of the dreadful creature, and he hurried them both to the door.

As Eddy looked back to apologize one last time, he could see that the cereal aisle was completely paved with bright-colored cereals. And the curious shoppers were tracking it all over the marketplace.

"I'm really sorry, Mr. Horton," Eddy said. "If there's anything I can do to help. . . ."

"Please, kid," Mr. Horton begged, giving Eddy a shove toward the door. "Just keep that horrid pet of yours away from my store. That's all I ask." Then Mr. Horton shut the door quickly and braced his back against it with a nervous sigh.

"Good work!" Eddy scolded the Grood. "Thanks to you and your big mess, I'll be giving my allowance to Mr. Horton for the rest of my life."

The Grood just stuck out its tongue and yanked rebelliously against the leash.

"Grood do what Grood WANT!" it whined. And it sat down to pout.

7
A Brief and Boisterous Bus Ride

Now that Eddy's bicycle was lying in a mangled heap beside the road, he had to figure out another way to reach Baxburg Aeronautics. And it had to be the fastest way possible because he had lost a lot of time in the grocery store. Indeed, the Grood was not making this trip easy at all. And with every second wasted, Uncle Sedrick was growing closer to fading from existence.

"All right, Grood!" Eddy said harshly. "I don't have enough money for a taxicab, so we're gonna have to take the bus. And you're gonna have to behave yourself, or we'll get kicked off. Got it?"

"Grood TIRED!" whined the Grood, tugging weakly on its new collar.

"That's okay," said Eddy. "You can sleep on the

bus. In fact, that would be perfect. But you've gotta stay in your seat, all right? No jumpin' around and buggin' people."

"Grood tum-tum HURT!" groaned the animal, clinging to its stomach again.

"Oh, brother," Eddy sighed.

The Grood was fairly well behaved at the bus stop. Most of the time, it lay sprawled out on the bench moaning and occasionally burping. Eddy was pleased to see that it would not be in the mood for troublemaking once they got on the bus. And in that case, they would probably make it to Baxburg Aeronautics in good time.

But as soon as the bus pulled up to the stop, the Grood came to life. The idea of going for a bus ride (being on a "FAST") thrilled the Grood into a terrible frenzy. And Eddy had to plead with the bus driver just to let him on board.

Eddy clutched the Grood against his chest and marched all the way to the back of the bus, hoping that the rear window view would occupy the Grood's attention. And it did for a while. But a few stops later, two elderly women boarded the bus and sat in the seat directly in front of Eddy. One of these women was wearing a large hat covered with plastic fruit. No sooner did the Grood see this than, of course, he wanted to eat the hat.

Unfortunately, Eddy did not foresee the oncoming disaster, and before he could react, the Grood

hopped from its seat and snatched the enticing fruit hat. The old lady let out a frightened scream and, along with her hat, off came her curly gray wig. And as the Grood bounced down the bus aisle, chewing on the plastic fruit, the whole bus load of passengers panicked. Some were frightened by the Grood; others thought that a fire had broken out; still others were simply afraid because of the general uproar.

Meanwhile, the Grood had made its way to the front of the bus where it was swinging round and round on a metal post. Eddy was trying to reach it, but the aisle was clogged up with screaming and scrambling people. As he tried to climb over bus seats toward the creature, he could see the latest developments. The Grood had grown bored of the metal post, and now it was interested in driving the bus. It bounced up to the driver's seat and grabbed onto the steering wheel with both furry hands. The poor bus driver had been searching for a place to stop the bus (due to all of the commotion on board), and the Grood added considerably to his problem.

The Grood clung to the steering wheel, howling and hooting and completely blocking the driver's vision. The bus careened wildly across the highway. Cars were honking angrily on every side, people were stomping and screaming in the aisle, and the nasty little Grood was fighting to keep control of the steering wheel.

PUTTFORD

At last, Eddy reached the front of the bus and ripped the Grood away from the dashboard. Instantly, it burst into rebellious screams, shouting, "FAST! Grood go FAST!"

The driver finally managed to stop the bus, turning onto someone's front lawn. His face was red as a radish and both of his hands were trembling frightfully. He wrenched the front doors open and pointed directly at the Grood.

"Get that THING out of my bus!" he cried. And Eddy obeyed immediately.

Dozens of angry faces appeared in the windows as the bus drove away.

It had been a terribly humiliating experience. But worst of all, Eddy now found himself standing on a sidewalk in a strange part of town with no way of getting to his destination.

"You're the stupidest, most rotten little creature that ever lived!" he screamed at the Grood. "You don't care about anyone but yourself, do you?!"

The Grood wasn't paying attention. It had just noticed an airplane flying overhead and was trying to jump up and grab it.

"Don't your realize that you're gonna be dead by tomorrow afternoon?" Eddy continued, quite pointlessly. "That's right! POOF! You'll be gone just like that. . . . And so will my Uncle Sedrick if we don't get some help pretty soon."

The Grood was not the least bit concerned. It held its fuzzy green arms out like two wings and tried to imitate the plane up in the sky. It ran to the end of its leash and jumped, thinking it would soar into the air. But of course, it fell straight to the ground with a *THUD*!, smacking its face on the ground. And there it sat, holding its nose and sobbing.

Eddy shook his head miserably. How could he possibly get through to this ridiculous animal? Couldn't it understand that he was only trying to *help* it?

8
The Grood Does Office Work

For the last half hour Eddy had been trying to get directions from people on the street. But the Grood behaved so atrociously that it scared everyone away. It would climb up people's legs or poke in their pockets or look through their shopping bags. And before they could give Eddy his directions, they would scurry off in fright.

It went on like this for quite a while and Eddy was growing more frustrated by the minute. He was also getting worried. It was growing late and Baxburg Aeronautics would be closing soon. And without the help of a scientist, there would be no way to save Uncle Sedrick.

Then, down the street came a very large man; he was walking an enormous bulldog on a leash.

Eddy figured that such a pair would certainly not be frightened off by anything so tiny as a Domestic Green Grood.

"All right, here comes someone!" Eddy told the Grood. "I'm going to ask him for directions, and I want you to leave him alone, do you hear me? And don't bother his dog either. A dog like that could chew you up for dinner. Are you listening?"

As the man and his dog approached, the Grood got down on all fours and tried to make a face like the bulldog. Eddy gave a tug on the leash to make the Grood stop, but it didn't.

"Excuse me, sir," Eddy said, stepping in front of the man. "I'm tryin' to find the Baxburg Aeronautics building. But I think I'm kinda lost."

"Say! That's some funny-lookin' monkey you got there, son," the man said with a smile. "Why'd you go and dye his hair all green like that?"

"Huh?" Eddy said, thrown off guard. "Oh . . . um . . . it just came that way. It's from a different country, sort of. But I was wonderin' . . . do you know where I can find Baxburg Aeronautics?"

"Why, sure," the man said, still chuckling at the Grood. "It's right up there on that hill." The man pointed to the hillside behind Eddy.

Eddy turned to see a big cluster of buildings perhaps half a mile away. He was greatly relieved to see they were so close.

"Hey, look," the man said, pointing down at the Grood and his bulldog. "My little Muffin and your

green monkey seem to like each other."

Up to this moment, the Grood had been crawling around and studying the bulldog, trying to copy its every move—panting, snorting, scratching for fleas, and so on. Just now the Grood was noticing the pug little tail on the bulldog's hind end. It was a fascinating little nob that simply begged to be touched. So the Grood reached out and grabbed it with a sharp tug. In a flash, the bulldog spun around and knocked the mischievous Grood to the ground. And before Eddy or the dog's owner could do anything, the bulldog stuffed the Grood's entire head inside its mouth. It held on tight and the Grood let out a frightened howl.

"Whoa there, Muffin!" the man shouted, slapping his dog's nose. "You let go of that critter!"

Eddy watched in horror as the Grood squealed and struggled between the monstrous jaws.

"Bad Muffin!" the man scolded. "Be nice to the monkey! Bad girl!"

But no amount of scolding would change the bulldog's mind. The only safe place for that Grood, the dog had decided, was inside its mouth.

"Well, don't that beat all," said the man, reaching into his pocket. He pulled out a piece of beef jerky. "Sometimes she gets like that, ol' Muffin does. Nothin' seems to change her mind but a nice chunk o' beef jerky."

The man waved the jerky in front of the bulldog's nose, and instantly it let go of the Grood. Then it sat down to chew on its snack as if nothing at all had happened.

The Grood, however, looked simply wretched. It was so frightened that its round pink face had turned a ghostly white, and its fur was sopping wet with dog drool. It sat down on the grass and began to bawl.

"Well, I'm awful sorry!" the man apologized. "My little Muffin's got a pow'rful hot temper. I sure hope she didn't squish your monkey too bad. Guess I better take her home and give her some vittles. Next thing you know she'll be chewin' on me."

The man waved and strode off down the sidewalk. Muffin trotted quietly along at his side.

"See what happens?" Eddy said, trying to calm the Grood by patting its head. "I told you not to bother that dog, didn't I? When are you gonna learn to listen to me?"

"Grood HURT!" howled the Grood. "Man BAD! Dog BAD!"

Eddy rolled his eyes in disgust.

After a great deal of soothing and comforting and pretending to feel sorry for the Grood, Eddy managed to get the creature back to its feet. It still fussed about wearing the leash (and about being hungry and tired and so forth), but at least it marched along willingly. Before too long, they had climbed the long drive and stood in a terrace outside Baxburg Aeronautics.

It was a gigantic complex: eight buildings in all, each of them big enough to house an airplane. Eddy decided to take the entrance that said INFORMATION above the doorway. But he was taking no chances this time. Before going into the building, he wrapped the Grood in his sweatshirt and tied a couple knots around it with the leash. Naturally, this put the Grood into an especially nasty fuss, so Eddy had to sit outside for another five minutes waiting for the creature to quiet down. At last, its throat got sore from screaming and its muscles got tired from struggling. Eddy picked up the Grood like a sack of potatoes and carried it into the lobby.

"All right, Grood," Eddy whispered. "If you behave yourself for a few more minutes then I'll untie you, okay? But if you do anything stupid, we're both gonna get thrown out of here, and you'll never get back to Planet Zerb! So you behave . . . *or else*!"

But, as usual, the Grood wasn't paying attention. It had noticed all the people sitting behind typewriters with their fingers dancing madly above the keyboards. The pinging of bells and the clattering of keys sent the Grood into an excited frenzy.

"Grood want *CLACK-CLACK*!" it cried, squeezing its arms out of the sweatshirt wrappings. "Grood go *CLACK-CLACK-CLACK! PING*!" And it wiggled its fingers over an invisible keyboard showing what it wanted to do.

"NO!" Eddy hissed. "You've got to behave! And I mean it this time!"

Eddy approached the reception desk and tried his hardest to look bright and friendly. He sorely wished he could leave the Grood behind, tied up to a chair or something, but the creature was the only way he could prove his story. So he stepped up to the desk nervously, clutching the Grood to his chest. Its fingers were still marching over imaginary typewriter keys as it said "CLACK-CLACK-PING!" over and over.

The receptionist looked up from her paperwork and gave a frightened start. It seemed for a moment as if she might faint.

"Hello, ma'am," Eddy said politely. "I'd like to see the Head Scientist, please."

"You . . . what? The Head Scientist?" the woman said, staring at the Grood nervously. "He's gone . . . or . . . that is . . . I think he's in a meeting. Is there . . . something I can do to . . . help you?"

The Grood's dramatics were increasing by the second. It had worked all of its top half out of captivity, and it was trying to reach for the receptionist's typewriter.

"No, I don't think so, ma'am," Eddy said, grabbing the Grood's arms. "I need somebody who understands how to fix space machines. See, my Uncle Sedrick got sent into outer space, and if I can't get him back by tomorrow at three o'clock, he'll disappear forever."

The woman's gaze never left the Grood. She had slid to the back of her chair, as far away as possible from the creature's prancing green fingers.

"I'm not makin' this up, ma'am," Eddy insisted. "See this animal I'm holdin'? It showed up in Uncle Sedrick's machine right after he got sent into space. It's a Domestic Green Grood from the Planet Zerbo-somethin'-or-other."

"Yes . . . I . . . I see," said the receptionist. "Perhaps I should have someone look into this. . . ."

She reached cautiously across her desk for the telephone, her eyes never leaving the strange beast that hovered above her desk.

Finally Eddy was getting somewhere. He felt incredibly relieved. For the first time during this whole catastrophe, the Grood hadn't managed to ruin everything. He leaned against the desk to rest his legs while the receptionist dialed the phone.

But before she could finish dialing, the Grood gave a sudden lurch and sprang from Eddy's arms onto the desktop. The receptionist let out a terrified shriek and jumped away from her desk. She turned to run, but a wastebasket tripped her up, and she fell to the carpet. The Grood instantly pounced on top of her typewriter and began hammering away on the keys.

CLACK-CLACK-CLACK . . . CHATTER-CHATTER . . . PING!

Eddy dove toward the Grood at once—but it dodged his grasp. And before he could make a second grab, it raced across the room like a furry green hurricane. It scrambled over desktops, upsetting

stacks of paperwork and knocking coffee mugs to the floor. People rose from their desks with shrieks and gasps. *CLACK-CLACK-PING*! sang the typewriters as the Grood bounced from one to the next. And just as a row of filing cabinets crashed to the carpet, three security guards burst into the room.

One of them grabbed Eddy, while the others chased down the Grood. Before Eddy had a chance to explain, he was lifted off the ground and rushed down the nearest corridor. Behind him, in a tossing, kicking, howling heap, came the beastly little Grood giving two security guards the fight of their life.

9
Eddy the Jailbird

By now all of the scientists at Baxburg Aeronautics had gone home. The only people left in the building were Eddy and the three security guards. As for the Grood, it was curled up at Eddy's feet, whimpering and chewing on its toenails. They were waiting for the police to arrive.

The security officers had called Eddy's house, but his parents weren't home, of course. And since he had no other friends or relatives in the area, he was going to be taken to the Puttford Home for Runaway Boys until his parents got back from England. Eddy had tried to explain his predicament, but no one would believe his story. In fact, the security guards were all convinced that the Grood was nothing more than a small boy dressed up in a green monster costume. They had tried to take the costume off the creature once, but it bit one of them on the nose and shrieked so loudly that they all got earaches. So they decided to leave the whole matter for the police.

About now, Eddy was feeling pretty miserable. An entire day had just gone by with nothing accomplished to help save Uncle Sedrick. Now it was nighttime, and Eddy was going to be locked up in a boys' home. If Eddy couldn't think of something *very soon* then Uncle Sedrick would be lost for sure. But what could possibly be done now, in the middle of the night? Especially when no one would even listen to his story?

One thing Eddy knew for sure. He would be of no use at all to Uncle Sedrick if he was locked up in a home for runaway boys. He had to get away . . . and he had to get away *now*, before the police showed up. Unfortunately, all three of the security guards were seated around a table that stood between Eddy and the doorway. They were in the middle of a card game, though, which meant they weren't paying all that much attention to their prisoners. And with a bit of scheming, Eddy soon came up with a plan to take advantage of the situation.

"Excuse me, officers," Eddy said, stepping up to the table. "I'm feeling kinda tired. Would it be okay if I took a nap on the floor till the police get here?"

"Sure, kid," said a guard with a red nose (it was red because the Grood had bitten him). "And tell your buddy there to quit chewing on his toenails, would ya? It's really disgusting."

"Yes, sir," Eddy said politely.

After a great performance of yawning and stretching, he made a pillow out of his sweatshirt and lay down at the foot of the table. The officers went on with their card game as Eddy pretended to fall asleep. He snorted a couple of times and smacked his lips just to make it look realistic. Then he began to inch his way underneath the table.

Lying facedown on the carpet, he dragged himself forward like a caterpillar, very slowly and very quietly. This was a painstaking procedure, but it worked. When he was done, Eddy had worked his way completely underneath the tabletop so that he was lying between all three pairs of shiny black shoes. Then, very carefully, he untied each guard's shoelaces and laid them out straight on the carpet. And finally, he gathered all the loose shoelaces together and tied them into one huge, tight knot. The card game went on without concern.

With the hardest part completed, Eddy worked his way out from under the table using the same caterpillar method, except going backwards. He continued his slow retreat until he had moved himself all the way back to the Grood, which was now curled up in a green ball, fast asleep. Then in one fast move, he swept the Grood up off the floor and raced for the door.

All three guards jumped to their feet in a flash.

But as they went to spring from the table, their shoelaces snapped tight and their feet came to a sudden stop. The whole bunch of them tumbled to the floor in an explosion of chairs and playing cards.

And before they could figure out what had happened, Eddy was out the door and charging down the hallway.

Fortunately, the building's front door was not locked from the inside. And while the guards were still trying to untangle their shoelaces, Eddy and the Grood raced out to the Baxburg parking lot. Two police cruisers were coming up the driveway at that same moment, and their headlights caught Eddy as he dove for the bushes at the edge of the parking lot.

"That must be him!" someone shouted just as a police car door flew open.

"Let's get him!" another voice cried.

Eddy plunged into the forest clutching the Grood under his arm. Nighttime had settled into the woods; only the last silver patches of twilight lit Eddy's way through the tangle of trees and underbrush. But this also worked in his favor, for the shadows engulfed him, making him invisible to the men on his trail. As he scampered up a rocky hillside, he could hear them rustling through the leaves below, and suddenly, a bright stream of light shot through the forest beside him—the policemen had flashlights! Then came a chorus of shouts, and three more flashlight beams. The security guards had freed themselves from Eddy's knot and now they were joining the hunt.

Eddy tried to keep low in order to dodge the searching flashlights. Since he was considerably smaller than the officers, he had been able to move much faster beneath the tree limbs. And it looked as if his escape was likely, but then the Grood began to fuss. It let out a desperate howl and struggled miserably in Eddy's arms.

"Over there!" came a voice. And several flashlights turned in Eddy's direction.

Eddy cupped his hand over the Grood's mouth and ran as fast as he could. He came to the edge of a meadow and changed directions, hoping to throw the officers off his trail. He ran downhill, almost backtracking, and found his way to a sheltered ravine. This was a wonderful turn of luck, for at the bottom of the ravine there was a loud, rushing stream which pounded over the hillside in a series of thundering waterfalls. Eddy found a dark hollow in the side of the ravine where he could hide, and he pulled the Grood inside, pinning it down in a corner.

Now, as the Grood kicked and squealed and made all the noise it could possibly make, the waterfall roared above it like a tireless drummer. Cry as it would, no one could hear its wretched little voice. And there they stayed for a very long time—but, as Eddy would later say, *any* time at all spent in the company of a Grood was a *very long* time indeed!

10
Smoke in the Woods

The moon was very little help that night. It was nothing but a dull orange cresent floating above the treetops. Eddy had to pick his way through the forest mostly by feel, which earned him far too many smacks in the face from twigs and bushes, and far too many bumps on the shins from fallen limbs. Altogether, the going was slow and painful.

And, as usual, the Grood was pathetic. Eddy had grown tired of carrying it and was trying to walk it on the leash. But it didn't cooperate. It dragged along behind him, clutching its neck and choking, frequently falling to the ground as if it were about to suffocate. Nonetheless, Eddy pushed on. He had picked out the North Star and decided to follow it until he came to civilization; after that, he didn't know what he'd do. Uncle Sedrick's time was running out.

For a brief moment, Eddy imagined that he could smell smoke—perhaps from a chimney or a campfire. And just as he stopped to get a better whiff, the Grood yanked the leash out of his hand and ran off into the forest. Eddy raced after it, and would soon have overtaken it, but suddenly it sprang into the air and scrambled up the side of a maple tree. Then it perched itself on a branch and began to cry.

"Grood HUNGRY!" it moaned. "Grood TIRED!"

"Aw, come on!" Eddy shouted up into the tree. "I know you're hungry and tired. So am I. But we gotta keep going. If we don't get some help then you're gonna die! And so will my uncle."

The Grood moaned horribly, sniffling and wheezing with self-pity. It wasn't listening at all.

"Please, Grood!" Eddy begged. "Just a little farther, that's all. We've gotta find someone to fix Uncle Sedrick's machine. We've only got a few more hours until . . ."

Eddy sat down at the foot of the tree, exhausted. It was completely useless to try reasoning with the Grood—it neither listened nor cared. Eddy's frustration had now gone beyond his human strength. He had tried to befriend the Grood—but it was too selfish to have friends. He had warned the Grood about dangers and getting in trouble—but it would never listen to anything but its own stubborn will. He had tried to explain to the Grood that it would die if they couldn't find help—but it was so concerned with getting what it wanted *now* that it couldn't understand when Eddy was trying to help it.

For the first time, Eddy had to admit to himself that there was absolutely no hope. If the Grood could not see what was good for itself, and would not listen to anyone else, then how could Eddy help save its life?

Eddy rested against the tree trunk and decided he would just stay there forever, since there was no hope at all in going on. Meanwhile the Grood whined and grumbled from the treetop.

Eddy had just closed his eyes for a moment when he thought he heard something. He was startled awake and, once again, he imagined that he could smell wood smoke on the wind. He stood and looked around. Yes, he was certain now—he could smell a fire somewhere nearby. And as he scanned the forest carefully, his eye caught an orange light flickering in the distant treetops.

"Hey, Grood!" Eddy shouted. "There's a camp fire over there! Look, out in the woods! There's people!"

"Grood HURT!" moaned the beast.

Eddy considered throwing rocks to knock the Grood out of the tree, but realized that he was letting his anger get the best of him. So he thought of a better plan.

"Hey, Grood," he said. "Want some FOOD?"

"Grood EAT!" shouted the Grood, suddenly coming to life.

"See that orange light off in the woods?" Eddy said. "That's a camp fire. That means there's people with FOOD over there."

The Grood sprang from the tree like a hawk after prey. It bore through the forest in a squealing fit of joy, with Eddy racing along behind it. The Grood was well ahead of Eddy when it broke out of the forest and came bounding into a large campsite. A couple dozen kids jumped to their feet screaming as the Grood charged through their village of pup tents and made its way to the nearest picnic table. Eddy burst onto the scene just in time to see the Grood plunge face first into a large cooler. When it emerged, its face was smeared with raspberry jam and it was chewing on a raw hot dog.

"No, Grood!" Eddy shouted, racing through the startled group of campers. "Bad Grood!"

He snatched the Grood out of the cooler, but it dragged the hot dog package along with it. The campers had now stopped screaming and they stared at Eddy and the Grood in stunned silence. All at once, Eddy realized that he knew these people—they were the kids from Camp Tomahawk. And out of the midst of them came Mrs. Pottswell, the nature counselor—Eddy's least favorite person in the whole world. But tonight she did not look quite as stern and terrible as usual. In fact, she

rather looked like she'd just met Count Dracula. She stared at Eddy, and then the Grood, with the most peculiar expression—her lips were pursed to speak long before the words came.

"Eddy?" she said at last. "Eddy Hooper, is that you?"

"Yes, ma'am," Eddy said politely, trying to pry the hot dogs from the Grood's fingers. "I didn't mean to startle you, Mrs. Pottswell . . . but I gotta tell you, I sure am glad to see you!"

"Well . . . yes . . . I see . . ." she stammered. "But what, may I ask, are *you* doing here? How did you ever find us?"

"I didn't mean to find you, ma'am," Eddy explained. "You see, it's like this . . . well, it's a long story. . . . I better explain the whole thing, Mrs. Pottswell."

And that's what Eddy did. He recounted his whole story from the day he was kicked out of Camp Tomahawk to the present moment. He explained how Uncle Sedrick had fallen into the Exchange Machine and had been sent to Planet Zerb, and how the Grood had shown up in his place. And then how he had tried to find a scientist to help fix his uncle's machine, but the Grood kept getting him in trouble. And finally, how the police and security guards had hunted them all through the forest till they were thoroughly lost. And now, by shear coincidence they had come upon Camp Tomahawk's camping trip.

"And that's the honest truth, Mrs. Pottswell," Eddy explained. "You've gotta help me . . . or else my Uncle Sedrick's gonna disintegrate. Please, Mrs. Pottswell?"

"Well, I don't know," said Mrs. Pottswell, suspiciously. "The whole story sounds a little funny to me. But on the other hand, I *am* a scientist, and I've never seen anything like this strange little animal you've got. A Grood you called it? Hmmm . . . yes, I suppose I'd better look into it. But if this is some sort of a prank . . ."

"Oh, no, it's not, Mrs. Pottswell!" Eddy cried. "Oh, thank you! You won't be sorry, I promise! We've gotta go right now. Uncle Sedrick's only got a few hours left!"

Fortunately, there were two other Camp Tomahawk counselors along on the trip, so Mrs. Pottswell was able to leave the kids for a while and check out Eddy's story. They had to take the camp bus, which was the worst possible place you could put a Grood. So Eddy wrapped it up in his sweatshirt and sat on top of it for the whole trip. He was going to save that Grood's life whether it liked it or not.

11
Uncle Sedrick's Sneakers

As soon as Mrs. Pottswell got one look at Uncle Sedrick's Interplanetary Object Exchange Machine, she knew that Eddy was telling the truth. The next problem was trying to fix the thing. Mrs. Pottswell was a science teacher, not an astronomer like Eddy's uncle. But still, she was a very bright woman with plenty of faith and courage. For the rest of the night and into the morning, she studied Uncle Sedrick's notes trying to learn how to operate the Exchange Machine. Eddy sat patiently at her side, and every time she had an idea, he followed her directions without question.

Finally, by early afternoon on Uncle Sedrick's "last day," Mrs. Pottswell understood the machine well enough to give it a try. Eddy held up the diagrams, while Mrs. Pottswell followed them carefully, turning each switch in the proper order. After about an hour and a half—and with everything checked and double-checked—Mrs. Pottswell announced that the Exchange Machine was set to go. She took a deep breath and flicked the ignition switch.

The chattering of machinery hissed into action, the green lights on the glass compartment began flashing, and the computer monitors showed that everything was functioning just as it should. Eddy and Mrs. Pottswell watched the empty glass case anxiously, praying that Uncle Sedrick would appear. But after several minutes and no sign of him, it was clear that something was amiss.

"What's wrong, Mrs. Pottswell?" Eddy asked, a little frightened. "Shouldn't he be here by now?"

"I'm not sure," she replied. "Maybe the people on Planet Zerb don't have their machine on. But, no, that can't be. They'd have to leave it on—this is your uncle's only hope."

"Maybe we're too late," Eddy began to despair. "Maybe he's already . . . gone. . . ."

"Don't give up yet, Eddy," Mrs. Pottswell said. She turned once again to Uncle Sedrick's notes. "We must be overlooking something, some tiny little thing."

Eddy looked up at the timer on the Exchange Machine. It was now 2:56 p.m.—which meant they only had four minutes left to save Uncle Sedrick.

"Think, Eddy!" Mrs. Pottswell said. "You've got to think hard. Try to remember every move your uncle made the last time he ran the machine."

"I don't know, Mrs. Pottswell," Eddy said feeling defeated. "I just don't remember very much."

"But what *do* you remember?" she persisted. "Anything at all?"

"Well . . ." Eddy said, straining to think back. "I know he pulled down that red lever just like you did and set those dealies there like you've got 'em and then he put the toy airplane inside the case and then . . ."

"Wait a minute!" cried Mrs. Pottswell. "What was that about the airplane?"

"He put it inside the big glass thingy," Eddy repeated. "You know, so there'd be something to exchange with Planet Zerb."

Then Eddy realized—that was the missing piece! There had to be something *inside* the glass case for the exchange to work.

"The Grood!" cried Mrs. Pottswell. "In all this fuss, we forgot to put the Grood inside the Transport Box!"

With only a minute left on the clock. Mrs. Pottswell snatched the Grood (which was now tied up in a box, howling), and dropped it into the glass compartment.

Instantly, the lights turned from green to flashing red. The machine screamed into action, hissing and whirring with electric energy.

"Oh, please, machine!" Eddy whispered. "Please work! Please let Uncle Sedrick be all right!"

"Come on now!" Mrs. Pottswell joined in.

They both stared at the Exchange Machine with wide, anxious eyes, their hands clasped together. On and on the noise increased, the red lights flickered violently.

And suddenly, there came a flash of white—and the next moment, the Grood and its box were gone. Then came a second flash. And there in the glass case appeared a pair of sneakers. They were Uncle Sedrick's sneakers. . . . But Uncle Sedrick was not in them.

Eddy gasped in horror. Mrs. Pottswell stared down with equal dismay. Something had gone

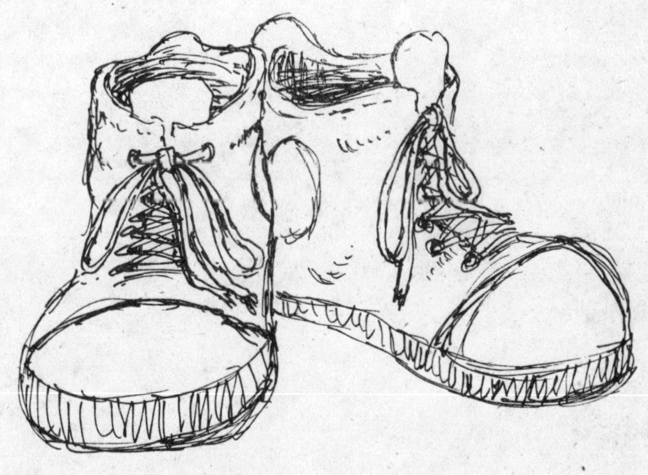

wrong. Where was Uncle Sedrick? Had they been too late? Was this all that was left of the poor old astronomer—nothing but a pair of sneakers?

Eddy dropped to his knees in front of the Transport Box and reached out to touch the empty shoes. He had tried so hard. He had done everything he could think of to save his uncle.

He fell to the floor and let the pain and weariness take him.

He had failed.

12

Earthquakes, Blue Shoes, and a Farewell Gift

As Eddy turned to stare at the empty Exchange Machine once again, he was suddenly reminded of the worst part of all. This whole mishap was *his* fault. If he had stayed in his seat that day, like he had promised Uncle Sedrick, none of this would have happened. And if he hadn't pulled down the ignition switch, the machine wouldn't have turned on, and Uncle Sedrick would still be right there, just as good as ever. This was a mistake for which Eddy would never be able to forgive himself.

And as he was thinking these things, clinging to Mrs. Pottswell, a soft rumbling noise came from somewhere outside the house. It slowly grew louder and the earth seemed to shake a little. *Maybe it's a thunderstorm*, Eddy thought. But the sky was clear.

Or it could be heat lightning, like the kind you get on humid nights. But it wasn't all that warm out. He looked up at Mrs. Pottswell and saw that she also heard the sound.

The rumble continued growing steadily until, finally, the house began to shake along with it. There was no other explanation. It had to be an earthquake.

"We better get out of here," Eddy suggested.

"Yes, I think we should," Mrs. Pottswell agreed.

They hurried down the stairs as chips of plaster crumbled from the ceiling. Pictures were falling from the walls and dishes toppled down from the pantry. The house had become a trembling blur by the time they reached the front hall. And suddenly, a strange glow streamed into the house, flooding in through every window.

Eddy threw open the front door and pulled Mrs. Pottswell out behind him. He was just about to start across the yard when, suddenly, the sky disappeared in a flash of white light. A second later, they were both knocked to the ground by a powerful gush of hot wind. They lay on the ground covering their eyes as the warm gust streamed over them. The glaring white light flooded the yard, erasing all shapes and colors so that only a blinding brightness filled the sky. There was no explanation for this at all—none that Eddy could think of.

Then, just as suddenly as it all had started, everything stopped. The blazing light dimmed to a soft blue, the hot wind died instantly with a gasping hiss, and there, hovering over Uncle Sedrick's lawn was an enormous spaceship. It was completely motionless, a silent giant shaped like an airborne seashell. Its blue lights twinkled softly in rhythmic formations, and its underside was enclosed in a sparkling pool of yellow electricity.

Slowly, Eddy lifted himself to his knees. He stared at the spaceship in fascination and horror. Mrs. Pottswell was a deathly white; she looked as though she had seen enough adventure for several lifetimes.

Then the silence was snapped. A silver hatch slid open in the spaceship's belly. Eddy braced himself, expecting some horrid space monster to come plunging out of the hole. But instead, there was a gentle, whirring sound and out of the opening came a long, silver shaft. It lowered all the way to the ground and rested gently on the grass. As soon as this was done, an egg-shaped vehicle—something like an elevator—came sliding down the shaft toward the ground. It came to a stop with the sudden *TING* of a bell, and a door popped open.

Then, out of the doorway hopped Uncle Sedrick.

Eddy and Mrs. Pottswell both jumped to their feet, stunned and delighted all at once. And Eddy, despite himself, burst into tears of joy.

Uncle Sedrick walked calmly across the yard, waving. Eddy charged toward him and almost plowed the old fellow to the ground with a ferocious hug. Even Mrs. Pottswell could not help but throw

her arms around the old astronomer.

Uncle Sedrick pulled himself free of Eddy and turned to wave to the spaceship. The silver shaft disappeared into the craft and the lights turned to a gleaming yellow. Then a voice came blasting out of the spaceship's loudspeakers.

"So long, Sedrick! Talk with you same time tomorrow. And please . . . . send the CAT this time! Ha ha ha!"

Another hot blast of air shot across the lawn, the high-pitched beep of a horn sounded, and, in little more than the blink of an eye, the spaceship was gone.

Eddy hugged his uncle once again.

"My goodness, Eddy," Uncle Sedrick said, trembling with excitement. "What a wonderful planet! You've never seen such a place! And oh, my, there's so much to tell you!"

"But I don't get it," Eddy said. "How come you didn't disintegrate or anything—you were gone for more than a day."

"Yes, indeed, it was a close one," Uncle Sedrick nodded. "It was tight up to the last minute. I must say I was getting awfully nervous waiting for you to switch on my machine and buzz me back to earth. I had to sit in Yibbig's Exchange Booth all night, you know. And when it got to be around noon in earth time, I completely gave up. I would've turned into *stardust* if not for good ol' Yibbig. He got this idea that he could take me home in his spaceship.

"Of course, he had no idea where earth was . . . not the foggiest! But he asked me a few questions about the earth's galaxy, and when I gave him a description of the Milky Way, he knew the exact solar system I was talking about. So we hopped into his spaceship and headed into space. Once he got me to the Milky Way, naturally I knew how to find earth from there. And so, here I am! Yibbig would've liked to stop and visit for a while, but he was a bit nervous that his spaceship might start to disintegrate. Ah, but that's all over with now. And I'll tell you, it sure feels good to be back home on planet earth."

"We had completely given up on you," Mrs. Pottswell said.

"Yeah," Eddy added, "especially when your sneakers showed up in the Exchange Machine —without *you* in 'em."

"You mean you didn't get my note?" said Uncle Sedrick.

"What note?" Eddy replied, and Mrs. Pottswell shook her head.

"The note that I put inside the sneakers," Uncle Sedrick explained. "I wrote you a note telling you not to worry, that I'd be returning to earth on Yibbig's spaceship. Then we put the sneakers inside Yibbig's Exchange Machine and left it on . . . just in case you figured out how to get my machine working."

Uncle Sedrick lifted up one of his feet displaying

the shoes he'd been given on Planet Zerb—a very odd pair indeed.

"Pretty nice, eh?" he chuckled. "They're dress shoes, of course."

Eddy and Mrs. Pottswell burst into laughter. They were the strangest-looking shoes you could ever imagine: shiny, blue things with pointy toes that curled round and round like a giant corkscrew.

"Well, if we'd only looked inside the sneakers!" laughed Mrs. Pottswell. "You sure gave us quite a scare."

"Yeah," said Eddy. "We thought you were a goner."

"Nope," Uncle Sedrick chuckled. "Good as ever. And the stories I have to tell now! I shall have to write a book . . . yes, indeed, I shall! An adventuresome yet scientific book. What should I call it? How about, *Zapped Up to Zerb*? No, no, that won't do . . . not academic enough. Perhaps, *Modern Communications with Extraterrestrial Hominids*. What do you think?"

"I think it's lovely," said Mrs. Pottswell. "And you must promise me that we can get together soon—I want to hear your stories in person. But now that today's emergency is over with, I'm afraid I have some campers to tend to."

"Campers?" said Uncle Sedrick.

"Yes," Mrs. Pottswell explained. "Eddy found me out in the middle of the woods. I was on an overnight trip with the kids from Camp Tomahawk.

And I think I'd better get back to the campsite—you know what mischief young people can cause!" She gave Eddy a teasing poke in the ribs.

"While we're on the subject of Camp Tomahawk," she added, "how would you like to come back to camp next week, Eddy? I do believe I've seen a change in you lately."

"Really?" cried Eddy. "You mean it?"

"Of course I do," Mrs. Pottswell chuckled. "As long as you don't bring that horrid Green Grood with you this time!"

"Green Grood?" said Uncle Sedrick. Eddy hadn't had a chance to tell him about the weird pet from Planet Zerb yet.

"I'll let Eddy explain *that* one to you," Mrs. Pottswell laughed.

Eddy and Uncle Sedrick walked to the back of the house with Mrs. Pottswell and watched her climb into the Camp Tomahawk bus. It grumbled to a start, and Eddy waved and shouted his thanks as she rolled down the driveway toward Puttford. He felt strangely sad to watch her leave. He imagined that he and Mrs. Pottswell would have become friends from the start if only he had given her a chance. . . . And, of course, if he hadn't dropped a snapping turtle into her favorite fish tank.

After the bus had disappeared over the crest of Bald Rock Hill, Eddy and Uncle Sedrick strolled back to the front yard and sat down on the doorstep.

Many things still needed to be explained, and Eddy was anxious to hear all about life on Planet Zerb.

"So, Eddy," Uncle Sedrick began. "Tell me about this animal that Yibbig sent us. A Green Grood you called it?"

"Yeah, a Domestic Green Grood!" Eddy exclaimed. "You wouldn't have believed it! It was the most horrible animal you could ever imagine. Some house pet! It wouldn't do a thing I told it to. And every time I turned around it was getting itself into trouble. We got thrown out of Horton's Grocery Store and kicked off the town bus. Then we got dragged away by security guards and chased through the woods by policemen. I kept trying to tell the Grood that it was gonna die it if didn't do what I said. But it didn't care. It kept saying *Grood do what Good want* and stuff like that. It was awful, Uncle Sedrick. You've got no idea just how awful it was!"

A grin spread across Uncle Sedrick's face. He stared at Eddy for a long while, his smile growing broader and broader. Then, finally, he broke into laughter, his entire body bouncing with amusement, almost knocking Eddy off the doorstep.

"Oh, Eddy!" he said at last. "I'm afraid I have to disagree with you—I think I know *exactly* what it's like to have a Domestic Green Grood around! As I recall, a fellow much like the one you just described pulled the ignition switch on my Exchange Machine and sent me flying into outer space!"

"Me?" said Eddy.

"Who else?" said Uncle Sedrick. "And the same young man was kicked out of camp just a few days earlier, I believe. Now what was the reason for that? Diving from a rooftop over three canoes, wasn't it? And shooting six arrows at a time, and putting a snapping turtle into a fish tank. Now, didn't you tell me that this Grood had no use for your rules and instructions, and it didn't even care that you were trying to protect it?"

Eddy was speechless. Until now, he had never imagined that he was anything like the Grood. And, frankly, it was not a pleasant feeling.

"Perhaps my friend Yibbig is an even wiser fellow than I had imagined," Uncle Sedrick went on. "Watching over that Grood must've been a little bit like doing God's job—watching over human beings. We're a lot like that Grood, you know. We're all so busy trying to *get* what we want, and trying to *do* what we want, that we never even notice the harm we're doing to ourselves—or how we might hurt other people. There's an awful lot to life that we can't see or understand. But God can. And we have to believe that He knows best, because if everyone made up their own rules, the world would be just like a roomful of Groods!"

Eddy grimaced at the idea of all those Groods.

"Yeah, all that stuff makes sense," he said. "But how are we supposed to know which rules are God's and which ones are just made up?"

"Well, it *is* true," Uncle Sedrick explained, "not all rules are good ones. And not all adults are good with authority. But the most important thing for you and me is *wanting* to please God. And that means listening when He speaks to your conscience—that little voice in the back of your head. See, this is why God gave us the Bible, and it's why He sent Jesus to live here on earth. He wanted us to know how to live happy lives and how to love other people. And lots of times, that means following rules and directions that we'd much rather ignore. But unless we want to go through life being as dangerous and obnoxious as that Grood, then we all have to show a bit of respect for each other. Do you see what I mean?"

"Yeah," said Eddy, "It's pretty easy to see that now—thanks to that dumb Grood and how it almost drove me nuts. I really *am* sorry about messing with your machine and sending you to Zerb, Uncle Sedrick. And the stuff at Camp Tomahawk, too . . . even though I really *was* just trying to have fun."

"Your apology is accepted," said Uncle Sedrick, offering his hand for Eddy to shake. "But you must understand, if you apologize for doing something, it means you don't plan to do it again."

"Don't worry, I promise," said Eddy. "If that guy, Yibbig, is gonna send you more stuff like that Grood, there's no way I want to be stuck here alone again!"

Uncle Sedrick laughed warmly, satisfied with Eddy's promise. He stood up to go inside and helped Eddy to his feet. But as Eddy stood, he noticed a dark object out in the center of the yard. It sat on the grass directly below the spot where the spaceship had been.

"What's that thing, Uncle Sedrick?" Eddy said, pointing.

"I don't know," Uncle Sedrick said. "Maybe we'd better go find out."

They crossed the yard toward the object, and as they drew closer, Eddy had a terrible feeling that he recognized the shape.

"Oh, no!" he said. "It can't be! Yibbig wouldn't do this to us!"

"What?" said Uncle Sedrick, a bit frightened. "What is it?"

And as Eddy pulled the cloth off the object, Uncle Sedrick could see for himself exactly what it was: A cage containing a Domestic Green Grood from Planet Zerb.

There was a note attached. This is what it said:

CORRESPONDENCE DATE: Vargomid 58th, Year of Kernik D#6792

TO: Dr. Sedrick F. Heisenburg of Planet Earth

Dear Sedrick,

Just before departing from your lovely

planet earth, I have decided to leave behind this charming pet Grood from Zerboglatus Five. Every boy on Zerb owns a Grood, and I thought your nephew Eddy might want one of his own.

There is something very strange about the Grood—although it can be a terribly huge nuisance and an altogether miserable pet, it has an amazing knack for keeping boys out of trouble.

So long for now. And more mud on your shoes than ever!

Your friend,

Yibbig of Planet Zerb

PS. You don't have to worry about the Grood disintegrating because I cloned it especially for you right here in earth's atmosphere. So you can expect it to live a good two or three hundred years. Enjoy!